The Mabinogion

A Phoenix Paperback

The Mabinogion was first published in Everyman's Library in 1949.
Revised and Reissued 1993.

Translation and introduction © Gwyn Jones and
Thomas Jones 1949, 1974, 1989, 1993

Cover illustration: 'Britomart and Amoret,' 1898,
by Mary F. Raphael (1889–1915),
© Christopher Wood Gallery, London/Bridgeman Art Library, London

This abridged edition published in 1996 by Phoenix
a division of Orion Books Ltd
Orion House, 5 Upper St Martin's Lane, London WC2H 9EA

ISBN 1 85799 639 9

Typeset by CentraCet Ltd, Cambridge
Printed in Great Britain by
Clays Ltd, St Ives plc

CONTENTS

The Lady of the Fountain

The emperor Arthur was at Caer Llion on Usk. He was sitting one day in his chamber, and with him Owein son of Urien and Cynon son of Clydno and Cei son of Cynyr, and Gwenhwyfar and her handmaidens sewing at a window. And although it was said that there was a porter to Arthur's court, there was none. Glewlwyd Mighty-grasp was there, however, with the rank of porter, to receive guests and far-comers, and to begin to do them honour, and to make known to them the ways and usage of the court: whoever had right to go to the hall or chamber, to make it known to him; whoever had right to a lodging, to make it known to him. And in the middle of the chamber floor the emperor Arthur was seated on a couch of fresh rushes, with a coverlet of yellow-red brocaded silk under him, and a cushion and its cover of red brocaded silk under his elbow.

Thereupon Arthur said, 'Sirs, if you would not make game of me,' said he, 'I would sleep while I wait for my meat. And for your part you can tell tales and get a stoup of mead and chops from Cei.' And the emperor slept.

And Cynon son of Clydno asked of Cei that which Arthur had promised them. 'But I,' said Cei, 'would have the good tale that was promised me.' 'Why, man,' said Cynon, 'it were fairer for thee to fulfil Arthur's promise first; and afterwards, the best tale we know, we will tell it thee.'

Cei went to the kitchen and the mead-cellar and brought with him a stoup of mead and a gold goblet, and his fist full of spits with chops on them. And they took the chops and began drinking the mead. 'Now,' said Cei, 'it is for you to pay me my story.' 'Cynon,' said Owein, 'pay Cei his story.' 'Faith,' said Cynon, 'an older man and a better teller of tales art thou than I. More hast thou seen of wondrous things. Do thou pay Cei his tale.' 'Start thou,' said Owein, 'with the most wondrous thing thou knowest.' 'I will,' said Cynon.

'I was the only son of my father and mother, and I was high-spirited, and great was my presumption, nor did I believe that there was any one in the world who might get the better of me at any kind of feat. And after I had mastered every feat that was in the same country as myself, I made me ready and travelled the bounds of the world and its wilderness. And at long last I came upon the fairest vale in the world, and trees of an equal height in it, and there was a river flowing through the vale, and a path alongside the river. And I travelled along the path till mid-day; and on the other side. I travelled till the hour of nones. And then I came to a great plain, and at the far end of the plain I could see a great shining castle, and a sea close to the castle. And I came towards the castle. And lo, two curly-yellow-headed youths, with a frontlet of gold about the head of each of them, and a tunic of yellow brocaded silk upon each of them, and two buskins of new cordwain upon the feet of each, and buckles of gold on their insteps fastening them. And a bow of ivory in the hand of each of them, and strings of deer sinews thereto, and arrows with their shafts of walrus-ivory, winged with peacocks' feathers, and heads of gold on the shafts. And gold-bladed knives, and their hilts with walrus-ivory in each of the two bosses, and they shooting at their knives. And some way off from them I could see a curly-yellow-headed man in his prime, with his beard new trimmed, and a tunic and mantle of yellow brocaded silk about him, and a ribbon of gold threaded in the mantle, and two buskins of speckled cordwain upon his feet, and two gold bosses fastening them.

'And when I saw him I drew near to him and greeted him, and so courteous were his manners that or ever I greeted him he had greeted me. And he accompanied me to the castle. And there was no sign of habitation in the castle, save what was in the hall. But there there were four-and-twenty maidens sewing brocaded silk by a window, and I tell thee this, Cei, that to my mind the least fair of them was fairer than the fairest maiden thou didst ever see in the Island of Britain. The least lovely of them, lovelier was she than Gwenhwyfar, Arthur's wife, when she was ever loveliest, Christmas day or Easter day at Mass. And they rose up to meet me, and six of them took my horse and drew off my boots, and six others of them took my arms and cleansed them in a rocker till they were as bright as what is brightest. And the third six laid cloths on the tables and set out food; and the fourth six drew off me my travelling garb and placed another garb upon me, namely, a girdle and trousers of bliant, and a tunic and surcoat and mantle of yellow brocaded silk, with a wide orfray on the mantle, and drew under me and around me cushions a-plenty with covers of red bliant. And then I sat me down. And the six of them that took my horse made him faultless in all his harness, as well as the best grooms in Britain. And thereupon, lo, silver bowls, and in them water to wash, and towels of white bliant, and some green; and we washed. And the man just mentioned went to sit at table, and I next to him, and the ladies below me, save for those who were serving. And the table was of silver, and of bliant was the table napery. And there was no one vessel served at table save gold or silver or buffalo-horn. And our meat came before us. And thou canst be sure, Cei, that I never saw nor heard tell of meat or drink whose like I saw not there, save that the service of meat and drink I saw there was better than in any place ever.

'And we ate till the meal was half over, and till then neither the man nor any of the maidens spoke a single word to me. And when the man judged it likely that I had rather converse than eat, he asked me what journey I was on and what kind of man I was. And I made answer that it was high time I had some one who would converse with me, and that there was not a fault at court so great as their being men so poor at conversation. "Why, chieftain," said the man, "we would have conversed with thee long since, save that it would have hindered thee in thy eating. But now we will converse with thee."

'And then I told the man who I was and the journey I was on, and I declared that I was seeking some one who might get the better of me or I get the better of him. And then the man looked on me and smiled 5 gently, and said to me, "Did I not believe that over-much mischief should come upon thee for my telling it thee, I would tell thee of that thou art seeking." And I felt grief and sadness come over me, and the man could see that by me, and said to me, "Since thou hadst rather," said he, "that I tell thee of thy hurt than of thy good, tell it I will. Sleep here tonight," said he, "and rise early and take the road thou camest up through the valley until thou enter the forest thou camest through, and some distance into the forest a by-way will meet thee on thy right, and journey along that until thou come to a great clearing as of a level field, and a mound in the middle of the clearing, and a big black man shalt thou see on the middle of the mound who is not smaller than two of the men of this world. And one foot has he, and one eye in his forehead's core; and he has a club of iron, and thou canst be sure that there are no two men who would not find their full load in the club. But his is not an ugly disposition; yet he is an ugly man, and he is keeper of that forest. And thou shalt see a thousand wild animals grazing about him. And ask him the way to go from the clearing, and he will be gruff with thee, but even so he will show thee a way whereby thou mayest have that thou art seeking."

6   'And that night was long to me. And on the morrow

early I rose and arrayed me, and mounted my horse and went my way through the valley and the forest, and I came to the by-way the man spoke of, even to the clearing. And when I came there, what wild animals I saw there were thrice as remarkable to me as the man had said; and the black man was sitting on top of the mound. Big the man told me he was: bigger by far was he than that. And the iron club in which the man had said was the full load of two men, I was sure, Cei, that there was therein the full load of four warriors. It was in the black man's hand. And I greeted the black man, but he spoke nothing to me save incivility. And I asked him what power he had over the animals. "I will show thee, little man," said he. And he took the club in his hand, and with it struck a stag a mighty blow till it gave out a mighty belling, and in answer to its belling wild animals came till they were as numerous as the stars in the firmament, so that there was scant room for me to stand in the clearing with them and all those serpents and lions and vipers and all kinds of animals. And he looked on them and bade them go graze. And then they bowed down their heads and did him obeisance, even as humble subjects would do to their lord.

'And he said to me, "Dost see then, little man, the power I have over these animals?" And then I asked 7 the way of him, and he was rough with me, but even so he asked me where I wanted to go, and I told him what kind of a man I was and what I was seeking, and he then showed me. "Take," said he, "the path to the head of the clearing, and climb the slope up yonder till thou come to its summit. And from there thou shalt see a vale like a great waterway; and in the middle of the vale thou shalt see a great tree with the tips of its branches greener than the greenest fir trees. And under that tree is a fountain, and beside the fountain is a marble slab, and on the slab there is a silver bowl fastened to a silver chain, so that they cannot be separated. And take up the bowl and throw a bowlful of water over the slab, and then thou wilt hear a great peal of thunder; and thou wilt fancy that heaven and earth are quaking with the peal. And after the peal there shall come a cold shower, and it will be hard for thee to bear that and live. And hailstones will it be, and after the shower there will be clear weather, but there shall not be one leaf on the tree that the shower will not have carried away. And thereupon a flight of birds shall come to alight on the tree, and never hast thou heard in thine own country a song so delightful as that they shall sing. And even when thou shalt be most enraptured with the song, thou shalt hear a great panting and groaning coming towards thee along the valley. And thereupon thou shalt see a knight on a pure black horse, and a garment of pure black brocaded silk about him, and a pennon of pure black bliant upon his spear. And he will fall on thee as briskly as he can. If thou flee before him, he will overtake thee; if, on the other hand, thou abide his coming, and thou on a horse, he will leave thee on foot. And if thou find not trouble there, thou needst not look for trouble as long as thou live."

'And I took the path till I came to the top of the hill, and from there I could see even as the black man had told me. And I came to beside the tree, and I could see the fountain beneath the tree, and the marble slab beside it, and the silver bowl fastened to the chain. And I took up the bowl and threw a bowlful of water over the slab; and thereupon lo, a peal of thunder coming, far greater than the black man had said; and after the peal the shower. And I was sure, Cei, that neither man nor beast of those the shower overtook would escape with his life. For never a hailstone of it would stop for skin nor flesh, till bone checked it. But I turned my horse's crupper to face the shower, and set the beak of my shield over my horse's head and mane, and the beaver over my own head, and in this wise I bore the shower. And as my life was at a point to depart my body, the shower came to an end. And when I looked at the tree there was not one leaf on it. And then the weather cleared. And thereupon, lo, the birds alighting on the tree and starting to sing; and I am sure, Cei, that never before nor since have I heard a song as delightful as that. And even when I was most enraptured, listening to the birds singing, lo, a panting coming along the valley towards me and saying to me, "Knight," it said, "what wouldst thou have of me? What harm have I done thee, that thou shouldst do to me and my dominion that which thou hast done to-day? Didst not know that to-day's shower has left alive in my dominions neither man nor beast of those it found out of doors?" And thereupon, lo, a knight on a pure black horse; and a pure black garment of brocaded silk about him, and an ensign of pure black bliant upon his lance. And I made an attack. And though that was a sharp encounter, it was not long before I was borne to the ground. And then the knight passed the shaft of his lance through my horse's bridle-rein, and away he went and the two horses with him, and left me there. As for me, the black man out of pride did not so much as fetter me, nor did he despoil me. And back I came, the way I had come before.

'And when I came to the clearing the black man was there, and I confess to thee, Cei, it is a wonder I did not melt into a liquid pool for shame at the mockery I got from the black man. And that night I came to the castle wherein we had been the night before. And I was made more welcome that night than the night before, and better was I fed, and I might have the conversation I desired from man and woman. But I found none to mention anything to me concerning my expedition to the fountain; nor did I mention it to any. And there I remained that night.

'And when I arose on the morrow, there was a tawny-black palfrey with a bright red mane on him, as red as lichen, all saddled ready. And after putting on my armour and leaving my blessing there, I came to my own court. And that horse I have still, in the stable yonder, and between me and God, Cei, I would still not exchange him for the best palfrey in the Island of Britain. And God knows, Cei, no man ever confessed against himself to a story of greater failure than this. And yet, how strange it seems to me that I have never heard tell, before or since, of any one who might know aught concerning this adventure, save as much as I have told, and how the root of this tale is in the dominions of the emperor Arthur without its being hit upon.'

'Why, sirs,' said Owein, 'were it not well to go and seek to hit upon that place?'

'By the hand of my friend,' said Cei, 'oft-times

wouldst thou speak with thy tongue what thou wouldst not perform in deed.'

'God knows,' said Gwenhwyfar, 'it were better thou wert hanged, Cei, than that thou utter words as slanderous as those to a man like Owein.'

'By the hand of my friend, lady,' said Cei, 'thou hast uttered no greater praise of Owein than I myself.'

And with that Arthur awoke and asked whether he had slept at all. 'Aye, lord,' said Owein, 'a while.'

'Is it time for us to go to table?'

'It is, lord,' said Owein.

Then the horn was sounded to wash. And the emperor and all his household went to their meat. And when meat was ended, Owein slipped away and came to his lodging and made ready his horse and arms.

And when he saw day on the morrow he donned his armour and mounted his horse and he went his way to the bounds of the world and desolate mountains. And at last he hit upon the valley that Cynon had told him of, so that he knew for sure it was the one. And he travelled along the valley by the side of the river; and the other side of the river he travelled until he came to the waterway. And he travelled the waterway till he could see the castle. And he came towards the castle. He could see the youths shooting at their knives in the place where Cynon had seen them, and the yellow-haired man who owned the castle standing near them. And when Owein was at point to greet the yellow-haired man the yellow-haired man greeted Owein.

And he came forward to the castle, and he could see a chamber in the castle; and when he came to the chamber he could see the maidens sewing brocaded silk in golden chairs. And more remarkable by far to Owein was their exceeding fairness and beauty than Cynon had declared to him. And they arose to serve Owein as they had served Cynon. And more remarkable was his repast to Owein than to Cynon.

And midway through the meal the yellow-haired man asked Owein what journey he was on. And Owein told him the whole of his quest. 'And seeking the knight who guards the fountain would I wish to be.' And the yellow-haired man smiled gently, and it was hard for him to tell Owein of that adventure, even as it had been hard for him to tell it to Cynon. Even so, he told Owein everything concerning it; and they went to sleep.

And on the morrow early the maidens had Owein's horse made ready, and Owein went on his way till he came to the clearing wherein the black man was. And more remarkable was the size of the black man to Owein than to Cynon. And Owein asked the way of the black man, and he told it. And Owein, like Cynon, followed the path till he came to beside the green tree, and he could see the fountain and the slab beside the fountain, and the bowl upon it; and Owein took up the bowl and threw a bowlful of water upon the slab. And thereupon, lo, the peal of thunder, and after the peal the shower. Greater by far were these than Cynon had said. And after the shower the sky lightened; and when Owein looked on the tree there was not one leaf upon it. And thereupon, lo, the birds alighting on the tree and singing. And even when Owein was most enraptured with the birds' song he could see a knight coming along the vale, and Owein received him and encountered him with spirit. And they broke their two lances, and drew their swords and smote at each other, and thereupon Owein struck the knight a blow through his helm, both mail-cap and bourgoyne coif, and through skin, flesh and bone till it wounded the brain. And then the black knight knew that he had received a mortal blow, and turned his horse's head and fled. And Owein pursued him. But Owein could not get near enough to strike him with his sword, though he was not far off from him.

And thereupon Owein could see a great shining city. And they came to the gate of the city. And the black knight was let in, and the portcullis was let down

upon Owein, and it struck him behind the hind-bow
of the saddle, so that the horse was cut in two, right
through him, and the rowels of the spurs close to
Owein's heels, and so that the gate descended to the
ground, and the rowels of the spurs and part of the
horse outside, and Owein and the rest of the horse
between the two gates. And the inner gate was closed,
so that Owein might not get away; and Owein was in
a quandary. And as Owein was thus, he could see
through the join of the gate a road facing him and a
row of houses either side of the road. And he could
see a maiden with yellow curling hair, with a frontlet
of gold on her head and a garment of yellow brocaded
silk about her, and two buskins of speckled cordwain
on her feet, and she coming towards the gate. And she
bade open. 'God knows, lady,' said Owein, 'it can no
more be opened to thee from here than thou canst
deliver me from there.' 'God knows,' said the maiden,
''twere great pity thou mightst not be delivered. And
it were only right for a woman to do thee a good turn.
God knows I never saw a better young man for a
woman than thou. Hadst thou a woman friend, best
of woman's friends wouldst thou be; hadst thou a
lady-love, best of lovers wouldst thou be. And so,' said
she, 'what deliverance I can for thee, that will I do.
Take this ring and put it on thy finger, and put this 15

stone in thy hand, and close thy fist over the stone; and so long as thou conceal it, it will conceal thee too. And when they of the castle give heed, they will come to fetch thee, to put thee to death because of the man. And when they see thee not, that will vex them. And I shall be on the horse-block yonder, awaiting thee, and thou shalt see me even though I shall not see thee. And come thou and place thy hand upon my shoulder, and then I shall know thou hast come to me. And the way I go thence, come thou with me.'

And with that she went away thence from Owein. And Owein did everything the maiden bade him. And with that the men from the court came to look for Owein to put him to death. But when they came to look for him they saw nothing save half the horse. And that vexed them. And Owein slipped away from their midst, and came to the maiden and placed his hand on her shoulder, and she set off and Owein along with her until they came to the door of a large fair upper chamber. And the maiden opened the chamber, and they came inside and closed the chamber. And Owein looked around the chamber, and there was not in the chamber one nail not coloured with precious colour, and there was not one panel without its different kind of golden image thereon.

And the maiden kindled a charcoal fire, and took a

silver bowl with water in it, and a towel of white
bliant on her shoulder, and gave Owein water to wash.
And she placed a silver table inlaid with gold before
him, and yellow bliant as a cloth thereon, and she
brought him his dinner. And Owein was certain that
he had never seen any kind of food of which he did
not there see plenty, save that the service of the food
he saw there was better than in any other place ever.
And he had never seen a place with so many rare
dishes of meat and drink as there. And there was never
a vessel from which he was served save vessels of silver
or gold.

And Owein ate and drank till it was late afternoon.
And thereupon, lo, they could hear a loud crying in
the castle; and Owein asked the maiden, 'What outcry
is this?' 'They are administering extreme unction to
the nobleman who owns the castle,' said the maiden.
And Owein went to sleep. And worthy of Arthur was
the excellence of the bed that the maiden made for
him, of scarlet and grey, and brocaded silk and sendal
and bliant. And towards midnight they could hear a
dreadful loud crying. 'What loud crying is this now?'
asked Owein. 'The nobleman who owns the castle has
but now died,' said the maiden. And after a while of
day they could hear an immeasurable loud lamenting
and outcry. And Owein asked the maiden, 'What

means this outcry?' 'The body of the nobleman who owns the castle is being borne to the church.'

And Owein arose and dressed himself and opened a chamber window and looked towards the city, and he saw neither limit nor bound to the hosts filling the streets, and they fully armed, and many ladies with them horsed and a-foot, and all the clerics of the city chanting. And it seemed to Owein that the air rang, so great was the outcry and the trumpets and the clerics chanting. And in the middle of that host he could see the bier, and a pall of white bliant thereon, and wax tapers burning in great numbers around it, and there was not one man carrying the bier of lower rank than a mighty baron.

And Owein was certain that he had never beheld a train so beautiful as that with brocaded silk and satin and sendal. And following that host he could see a yellow-haired lady with her hair over her shoulders, and many a gout of blood on her tresses, and a torn garment of yellow brocaded silk about her, and two buskins of speckled cordwain upon her feet. And it was a marvel that the ends of her fingers were not maimed, so hard did she beat her two hands together. And Owein was certain that he had never beheld a lady as lovely as she, were she in her right guise. And

louder was her shrieking than what there was of man

and horn in the host. And when he beheld the lady he was fired with love of her, till each part of him was filled therewith. And Owein asked the maiden who the lady was. 'God knows,' said the maiden, 'a lady of whom it may be said that she is the fairest of women, and the most chaste, and the most generous, and the wisest and noblest. My mistress is she, and the Lady of the Fountain is she called, wife to the man thou slewest yesterday.' 'God knows of me,' said Owein, 'she is the lady I love best.' 'God knows,' said the maiden, 'she loves not thee, neither a little nor at all.'

And thereupon the maiden arose and kindled a charcoal fire, and filled a pot with water and set it to warm, and took a towel of white bliant and placed it round Owein's neck; and she took an ivory ewer and a silver bowl and filled it with warm water and washed Owein's head; and then she opened a wooden case and drew out a razor with its haft of ivory and two gold channellings on the razor. And she shaved his beard and dried his head and neck with the towel.

And then the maiden set up a table before Owein and brought him his dinner. And Owein was certain that never had he a dinner so choice as that, nor one more lavishly served. And when he had finished his dinner the maiden made ready the bed. 'Come hither,' 19

said she, 'to sleep. And I will go a-wooing for thee.'
And Owein went to sleep.

And the maiden closed the door of the upper
chamber and went towards the castle. And when she
came there, naught else was there save sadness and
care, and the countess herself in the chamber, not
bearing to see a soul for her sadness. And Luned came
to her and greeted her; but the countess made her no
answer. And the maiden was angered and said to her,
'What has come over thee that thou hast an answer
for no one to-day?' 'Luned,' said the countess, 'what a
face hast thou, not to come and show respect to the
grief that was mine! And yet I made thee wealthy. And
that was wrong of thee.' 'Faith,' said Luned, 'I did not
think but that thy good sense might be better than it
is. It were better for thee to seek and study to make
good the loss of that nobleman than something else
thou mayest never obtain.' 'Between me and God,'
said the countess, 'I could never make good the loss of
my lord in any other man in the world.' 'Thou
couldst,' said Luned, 'take as husband a man who
would be as good as, or better than he.' 'Between me
and God,' said the countess, 'were it not repugnant to
me to have put to death a creature I myself reared, I
would have thee put to death for suggesting to me a
thing so disloyal as that. But banished I will have

thee!' 'I am glad,' said Luned, 'that thou hast no reason for this save that I have told thee thine own good, where thou couldst not thyself hit on it. And shame on whichever of us first sends to the other, whether it be I to seek invitation of thee, or thou to invite me.'

And thereupon Luned made off, and the countess arose and went to the chamber door after Luned, and coughed loudly, and Luned looked back. And the countess gave Luned a nod, and Luned came back to the countess. 'Between me and God,' said the countess to Luned, 'evil is thy nature. But since it was my own good thou wast telling me, show me what way that might be.' 'I will,' said she.

'Thou knowest that thy dominions cannot be defended save by main strength and arms; and for that reason seek quickly one who may defend them.' 'How can I do that?' asked the countess. 'I will show thee,' said Luned. 'Unless thou canst defend the fountain thou canst not defend thy dominions. There is none can defend the fountain save one of Arthur's household; and I shall go,' said Luned, 'to Arthur's court. And shame on me,' said she, 'if I come away thence without a warrior who will keep the fountain as well or better than the man who kept it of yore.' 'That is not easy,' said the countess, 'but nonetheless go thou and put to the test that thou dost speak of.'

Luned set out under pretence of going to Arthur's court. And she came to the upper chamber to Owein; and there she remained along with Owein till it was time for her to have come from Arthur's court. And then she arrayed herself and came to see the countess. And the countess welcomed her. 'Thou hast news from Arthur's court?' asked the countess. 'The best news that I have, lady,' said she, 'is that I have prospered in my mission. And when wouldst thou have shown to thee the chieftain who has come with me?' 'Towards mid-day to-morrow,' said the countess, 'bring him to see me. And I shall have the town emptied against that time.'

And she came home. And towards mid-day on the morrow Owein put on a tunic and surcoat and a mantle of yellow brocaded silk, and a wide orfray of gold thread in the mantle, and two buskins of speckled cordwain on his feet, and the image of a golden lion fastening them. And they came to the countess's chamber; and the countess welcomed them. And the countess looked hard at Owein. 'Luned,' said she, 'this chieftain has not the look of a traveller.' 'What harm is there in that, lady?' asked Luned. 'Between me and God,' said the countess, 'that no man reft my lord's life from his body save this man.' 'All the better for thee, lady. Had he not been doughtier than he, he would not have taken his life. Nothing can be done in that affair,' said she, 'for it is over and done with.' 'Get you home,' said the countess, 'and as for me, I shall take counsel.'

And on the morrow the countess had the whole of her dominions summoned to one place, and she made known to them how her earldom was voided and might not be defended save by horse and arms and main strength. 'And I lay this choice before you: either do one of you take me, or let me take a husband from elsewhere who will defend it.'

They determined by their counsel to let her take a husband from elsewhere. And then she brought bishops and archbishops to her court to solemnize the marriage between her and Owein. And the men of the earldom did Owein homage. And Owein kept the fountain with spear and sword. This is how he kept it: whatever knight came there, Owein would overthrow them and hold them to ransom for their full worth; and that wealth Owein distributed amongst his barons and knights, so that his dominions had not love for a man in the whole world greater than their love for him. And three years was he thus.

And as Gwalchmei was one day walking with the emperor Arthur, he looked on Arthur and saw him sad and dejected. And Gwalchmei was much grieved to see Arthur in that state. And he asked him, 'Lord,' said he, what has befallen thee?' 'Between me and God, Gwalchmei,' said Arthur, 'there is longing upon me for Owein, who has been lost to me the space of three years, and if I be the fourth year without sight of him my life will not stay in my body. And I know for certain that it is because of Cynon's tale, son of Clydno, that Owein has been lost.' 'There is no need for thee, lord,' said Gwalchmei, 'to muster thy dominions to that end; but thou and the men of thy court may avenge Owein if he has been slain, or set him free if he is in prison. Or, if he be alive, bring him back with thee.' And what Gwalchmei said was determined on.

And Arthur went on his way, equipped with horses and arms, and the men of his household with him, to seek Owein. The number of his host was three thousand, not counting camp followers, and Cynon son of Clydno was guide to him. And Arthur came to the castle where Cynon had been. And when they came thither the youths were in the same place shooting, and the yellow-haired man standing near them. And
when the yellow-haired man saw Arthur he greeted

him and invited him, and Arthur accepted the invitation. And they proceeded to the castle. And although their host was a great one, their presence was not felt in the castle. And the maidens arose to serve them; and ever had they seen fault in every service save the service of the ladies. And no worse was the service for the grooms that night than would be for Arthur in his own court.

On the morrow early Arthur set out thence, with Cynon as his guide. And they came to where the black man was, and more remarkable by far to Arthur was the size of the black man than had been told him. And they came to the top of the hill, and to the vale beside the green tree, and till they saw the fountain and the bowl and the slab. And then Cei came to Arthur and said, 'Lord,' said he, 'I know the meaning of all this adventure, and it is my plea that I be allowed to throw the water on the slab and to bear the first disadventure that may come.' And Arthur granted this.

And Cei threw a bowlful of the water upon the slab. And straight thereafter came the peal of thunder, and after the peal the shower; and they had never heard a peal of thunder and a shower like to those. And many camp followers who were in Arthur's train the shower slew. And after the shower had left off the sky lightened; and when they looked on the tree there was not one leaf thereon. And the birds alighted on the tree; and certain were they that they had never heard a song so delightful as the birds' singing. And thereupon they could see a knight on a pure black horse, and a garment of pure black brocaded silk about him, and coming briskly. And Cei encountered him and jousted with him. And not long was the jousting ere Cei was thrown. And then the knight pitched his tent, and Arthur and his host pitched their tents that night.

And next day when they arose in the morning there was the signal for combat upon the knight's lance. And Cei came to Arthur and said to him, 'Lord,' said he, 'unfairly was I overthrown yesterday. And would it please thee that I go to-day to joust with the knight?' 'I give thee leave,' said Arthur. And Cei made for the knight, and straightway he threw Cei, and he looked on him and struck him on the forehead with the butt of his lance, so that his helm and the mail-cap were broken, and the skin and the flesh to the bone as wide as the head of the lance. And Cei came back to his comrades.

And thenceforward Arthur's retinue went each in his turn to joust with the knight, till there was none not thrown by the knight save Arthur and Gwalchmei.

And Arthur arrayed him to go and joust with the knight. 'Alas, lord,' said Gwalchmei, 'give me leave to go and joust with the knight first.' And Arthur gave him leave. And he went to joust with the knight, and a cloak of brocaded silk which the earl of Anjou's daughter had sent him about him and his horse. By reason of that, none from the host recognized him. And they charged each other and jousted that day till eventide, and neither of them was near throwing the other to the ground.

And on the morrow they went to joust, and keen lances with them, but neither of them vanquished the other. And the third day they went to joust, and strong stout keen lances with each of them. And they were fired with rage, and on the very stroke of noon they charged, and each of them gave the other such a thrust that all the girths of their horses were broken, and so that each of them was over his horse's crupper to the ground. And they arose quickly and drew their swords and laid on; and the host that beheld them thus felt certain that never had they seen two men as valorous as those, or as strong. And were the night dark, it would be light with the fire from their arms. And thereupon the knight gave Gwalchmei such a blow that the helm turned from off his face, so that the knight knew he was Gwalchmei. And then Owein said, 'Lord Gwalchmei, I knew thee not by reason of thy cloak – and thou art my first cousin. Take thou 27 my sword, and my armour.' 'Thou, Owein, art master,' said Gwalchmei, 'and thine is the victory. Take thou my armour.' And thereupon Arthur perceived them, and he came to them. 'Lord,' said Gwalchmei, 'here is Owein hath vanquished me and will not take my armour from me.' 'Lord,' said Owein, ''tis he that vanquished me and will not take my sword.' 'Give me your swords,' said Arthur, 'and then neither of you has vanquished the other.' And Owein threw his arms around the emperor Arthur's neck, and they embraced. And with that his host came pressing and hurrying towards them to try and see Owein and embrace him, and very nearly were there dead men in that press.

And that night all went to their tents. And on the morrow the emperor Arthur sought to depart. 'Lord,' said Owein, 'that would not be right of thee. Three years ago I came away from there, lord, and this place is mine, and from that day to this I have been preparing a feast for thee, for I knew thou wouldst come to look for me. And thou shalt come with me to rid thee of thy weariness, thou and thy men. And a bath you shall have.'

And they all came together to the castle of the Lady of the Fountain. And the feast that had been three years preparing was consumed in just three months.

And never had they a feast more cheering than that, nor a better. And then Arthur sought to depart. And Arthur sent messengers to the countess, asking her to allow Owein to go with him to be shown to the noblemen of the Island of Britain and their good ladies for just three months. And the countess gave him her consent, but she found it hard.

And Owein came with Arthur to the Island of Britain. And after his coming amongst his kindred and his boon-companions, he remained three years instead of three months.

And as Owein was one day eating at table in the emperor Arthur's court at Caer Llion on Usk, lo, a maiden coming on a crisp-maned bay horse, and its mane reached to the ground, and a garment of yellow brocaded silk about her, and the bridle and what might be seen of the saddle was all of gold. And she came up to Owein and took away the ring that was upon his hand. 'Thus,' said she, 'does one do to a false treacherous deceiver, to bring shame on thy beard.' And she turned her horse's head and away.

And then remembrance of his adventure came to Owein, and he was sorrowful. And when he had finished eating he came to his lodging, and he was troubled greatly that night. And on the morrow early he arose, 29 and it was not for Arthur's court that he made but the bounds of the world and desolate mountains. And he was wandering thus till his clothes perished, and till his body was nigh perished, and till long hair grew all over his body; and he would keep company with wild beasts and feed with them till they were used to him. And therewith he grew so weak that he might not keep up with them. And he came down from the mountains into the vale, and made for a park, the fairest in the world, and a widowed countess owned the park.

And one day the countess and her handmaidens went walking beside a lake that was in the park, until level with its centre. And they could see in the park the shape and likeness of a man. And they became as it were terrified of him. But nevertheless they drew near him, and felt him, and regarded him closely. They could see the veins throbbing on him, and he himself moaning because of the sun. And the countess returned to the castle and took a jar of precious ointment and placed it in her maiden's hand. 'Go,' said she, 'and this with thee, and take yonder horse and the garments with thee, and set them near the man back there. And anoint him with this ointment, next his heart, and if there be life in him he will arise with this ointment. And watch what he will do.'

And the maiden came her way and applied all the

ointment to him, and left the horse and the garments near at hand, and withdrew and went a little off from him, and hid and kept watch on him. And after a while she could see him scratching his arms and raising himself up and looking on his flesh, and he grew ashamed, so ugly did he see the appearance that was on him. And he perceived the horse and the garments a short way off from him, and he crawled until he reached the garments, and he drew them to him from the saddle and donned them, and with difficulty mounted the horse. And then the maiden revealed herself to him, and greeted him. And he welcomed the maiden, and he asked the maiden what land was that, and what place. 'Faith,' said the maiden, 'a widowed countess owns the castle yonder. And when her lord died he left her with two earldoms, but there is naught to her name this night save the one house yonder which the young earl who is her neighbour has not taken, because she would not go to him as wife.' 'That is pity,' said Owein; and Owein and the maiden went to the castle, and Owein alighted at the castle, and the maiden led him to a comfortable chamber and kindled a fire for him, and left him there.

And the maiden came to the countess, and placed the jar in her hand. 'Maiden,' said the countess, 'where is all the ointment?' 'It is gone, lady,' said she.

'Maiden,' said the countess, 'it is not easy for me to blame thee. But it was unfortunate for me that the sevenscore pounds' worth of precious ointment should be used up on a man without knowing who he is. But nonetheless, maiden, see to his needs so that he lacks for nothing.'

And that the maiden did, furnishing him with meat and drink and fire and bed and bath till he was whole. And the hair fell away from Owein in scaly tufts. Three months was he undergoing this, and his flesh was then whiter than before.

And thereupon, one day, Owein could hear a commotion in the castle, and a great preparation, and arms being fetched in. And Owein asked the maiden, 'What commotion is this?' asked he. 'The earl of whom I told thee,' said she, 'is coming against the castle to try and ruin this lady, and a great host with him.' And then Owein asked the maiden, 'Has the countess a horse and arms?' 'Even so,' said the maiden, 'the best in the world.' 'Wilt thou go to the countess to request the loan of a horse and arms for me,' asked Owein, 'so that I might go to look on the host?' 'I will, gladly,' said the maiden.

And the maiden came to the countess and told her all that he had said. Then the countess laughed. 'Between me and God,' said she, 'I will give him a horse and arms for ever; and never has he had to his name a horse and arms better than they; and it pleases me that he should accept them, lest to-morrow they be taken by my enemies against my will. But I know not what he wants with them.'

And a handsome black gascon was brought, with a beechen saddle on him, and arms ample for man and horse. And he arrayed himself and mounted the horse and set off, and two squires with him, equipped with horses and arms. And as they came towards the earl's host they saw neither bound nor limit to it. And Owein asked the squires which troop the earl was in. 'In the troop,' said they, 'in which are those four yellow standards yonder. Two are in his van, and two in his rear.' 'Aye,' said Owein, 'get you back and wait for me in the castle gateway.' And they returned. And Owein proceeded through the two foremost troops, till he encountered the earl. And Owein dragged him from his saddle, so that he was between him and his saddlebow, and he turned his horse's head towards the castle. And whatever trouble he had, he brought the earl along with him till he came to the castle gate where the squires were waiting for him. And in they came, and Owein made over the earl as a gift to the countess, and spoke to her thus: 'See here a return for the blessed ointment I had of thee.'

And the host pitched its tents around the castle. And in return for life given to the earl he gave back to her the two earldoms; and in return for his liberty he gave up the half of his own dominions, and the whole of her silver and gold and her jewels, and sureties to that end.

And away went Owein, and the countess offered him a welcome, him and the whole of his dominions; but Owein desired nothing save to travel the bounds of the world and its wilderness.

And as he travelled in this wise he heard a loud roaring within a forest, and a second, and a third. And he came thither, and when he had come he could see a huge craggy hill in the middle of the forest, and a grey rock in the side of the hill; and there was a cleft in the rock, and in the cleft was a serpent, and beside the serpent was a pure white lion, and when the lion tried to get away thence the serpent would make a dart at him, and then he would give a roar. Then Owein unsheathed his sword and drew nigh to the rock; and as the serpent was coming from the rock Owein cut at it with the sword till it was in two halves on the ground. And he came to the road as before. He could see the lion following him and sporting about him like a greyhound he had himself reared.

And they travelled throughout the day till eventide.

And when Owein thought it time to rest he dismounted and let his horse graze in a level wooded meadow. And Owein kindled a fire; and by the time Owein had the fire ready, the lion had enough firewood to last three nights. And the lion slipped away from him, and straightway, lo, the lion coming towards him with a fine big roebuck. And he dropped it in front of Owein and went to lie down between him and the fire.

And Owein took the roebuck and flayed it, and set chops on spits around the fire, and he gave the whole of the buck else to the lion to eat. And as Owein was about this he heard a loud moan, and a second and a third, and that nigh to him. And Owein asked whether it was any one of this world who made that. 'Aye, to be sure,' said the creature. 'Who art thou then?' asked Owein. 'Faith,' said she, 'I am Luned, the handmaiden of the Lady of the Fountain.' 'What dost thou there?' asked Owein. 'I am being kept in durance,' said she, 'by reason of a young man who came from the emperor's court and was with her a while. And he went to visit Arthur's court and never came back. And such a friend was he to me, I loved him best of the whole world. Two of the countess's chamberlains made mock of him in my presence and called him false deceiver. I made answer that their two bodies might not contend against his body alone, and for that they imprisoned me in this vessel of stone, and declared that life should not stay in my body unless he came to defend me by a set day. And the day set was not later than the day after to-morrow. And I have none to seek for him. Owein was he, son of Urien.' 'And wouldst thou feel sure,' was his answer, 'that if that young man knew of this, he would come to defend thee?' 'Sure, between me and God,' said she.

And when the chops were cooked enough, Owein divided them into two halves between him and the maiden. And they ate, and after that they conversed till it was day on the morrow. And on the morrow Owein asked the maiden whether there was a place where he might get food and welcome that night. 'There is, lord,' said she. 'Go through there,' said she, 'to the ford, and take the road alongside the river, and after a while thou wilt see a great castle with many towers thereon; and the earl who owns that castle is the best man in the world for food, and there thou canst spend to-night.'

And no watchman ever watched over his lord as well as the lion watched over Owein the night before.

And then Owein accoutred his horse and journeyed forward through the ford till he saw the castle. And
Owein came to the castle. And he was honourably

received there, and his horse amply attended to, and plenty of fodder set before it. And the lion went to the horse's stall to lie down, so that none from the castle might dare go near the horse because of him. And Owein was certain that he had never seen a place whose service was as good as that; but each man there was as sad as if death were on each man of them. And they went to meat, and the earl sat on Owein's one hand, and an only daughter he had on Owein's other side. And Owein was certain that he had never beheld any maiden more lovely than she. And the lion came to between Owein's two feet, under the table; and Owein fed it with every dish that was for himself. And Owein saw no fault there so great as the men's sadness.

And midway through the meal the earl bade Owein welcome. 'It was high time for thee to show cheer,' said Owein. 'God knows of us that it is not towards thee we are sad, but that a cause for sadness and care has befallen us.' 'What is that?' asked Owein. 'Two sons had I, and yesterday my two sons went to the mountain to hunt. There is a savage monster there, and he kills men and devours them. And he has caught my sons. And to-morrow is the day set between him and me, to hand over that maiden to him or that he kill my sons before my eyes. And there is the semblance of a man upon him, but he is not smaller than a giant.'

'Faith,' said Owein, 'that is pity. And which of those wilt thou do?' 'God knows,' said the earl, 'I judge it less shameful that my sons whom he got against my will should be slain than that my daughter be freely given him to be violated and slain.' And they talked of other matters. And Owein remained there that night.

And on the morrow early they heard a commotion great past telling. That was the big man coming, and the two boys with him. And the earl resolved to defend the castle against him and to abandon his two sons. Owein donned his armour and went out and pitted himself against the man, and the lion at his heels. And when the man saw Owein in arms he rushed at him and fought with him. And better by far did the lion fight against the big man than Owein. 'Between me and God,' said the man to Owein, 'I should not be hard put to it to fight with thee, were not the animal with thee.' And with that Owein drove the lion back into the castle, and fastened the gate upon him, and he came to fight as before against the big man. And the lion roared to realize Owein's plight. And he climbed till he was on the earl's hall, and from the hall on to the rampart, and from the rampart he leapt till he was with Owein. And the lion struck with his paw on the big man's shoulder till his paw was out through his fork, so that all his bowels might be seen slipping from him. And then the big man fell dead. And then Owein restored his two sons to the earl, and the earl offered Owein a welcome. But Owein would not have it, and came on to the meadow where Luned was.

And there he could see a great blaze of fire, and two handsome auburn curly-headed youths taking the maiden to throw her into the fire. And Owein asked what complaint they had against the maiden. And they told him their story, even as the maiden had told it the night before. 'And Owein has failed her, and therefore we will burn her.' 'Faith,' said Owein, 'that was a good knight, and I should marvel he had not come to defend her, had he known how it was with the maiden. And if you would have me go in his stead, why then I would for you.' 'That we will,' said the youths, 'by Him who made us!'

And they came to blows with Owein, and he was in sore straits with the two youths. And thereupon the lion came to Owein's assistance, and they got the better of the youths. And then they said, 'Ah, chieftain, it was not our compact to fight save with thee alone; and it is harder for us to fight with yonder animal than with thee.' And then Owein put the lion in the place where the maiden had been in durance, and made a wall of stones against the door, and went to fight with 39 the men as before. And Owein had not yet come to his strength, and the two youths pressed him hard, and the lion roaring all the while because Owein was in sore straits. And the lion tore down the wall till he found a way out, and quickly he slew one of the youths, and straightway he slew the other. And in this wise they saved Luned from being burned.

And then Owein, and Luned with him, went to the dominions of the Lady of the Fountain. And when he came away thence he brought the lady with him to Arthur's court, and she was his wife so long as she lived.

And then he came his way to the court of the Black Oppressor, and fought with him; and the lion did not leave Owein till he had vanquished the Black Oppressor. And when he came his way to the Black Oppressor's court, he made for the hall, and there he beheld four-and-twenty of the fairest ladies that any one had ever seen. But the raiment upon them was not worth four-and-twenty silver pennies; and they were sad as death. And Owein asked them the reason for their sadness. They said that they were the daughters of earls, and that they had not come thither save in company with him each one of them loved best. 'And

when we came here we received joy and honour, and

were made drunk. And when we were drunk the devil who owns this court came and slew all our husbands, and took away our horses and our raiment and our gold and our silver. And the bodies of the men are in this very house, and many corpses along with them. And there for thee, chieftain, the reason for our sadness. And we are grieved, chieftain, that thou too art come hither, lest ill befall thee.'

And Owein was grieved thereat, and he went to go walking outside. And he saw a knight coming towards him and receiving him with joy and affection, as though he were his brother. That was the Black Oppressor. 'God knows,' said Owein, ''twas not to win thy favour I came hither.' 'God knows,' replied he, 'thou wilt not get it then.'

And straightway they made for each other and encountered furiously. And Owein put forth his strength against him, and bound him with his hands behind his back. And the Black Oppressor asked Owein for quarter, and said to him, 'Lord Owein,' said he, 'there was a prophecy that thou shouldst come hither to subdue me; and come thou hast, and that thou hast done. And a despoiler was I here, and a house of spoil was my house; but grant me my life and I will become a hospitaller, and I will maintain this house as a hospice for weak and for strong so long as 41

I live, for thy soul's sake.' And Owein accepted that of him. And Owein remained there that night.

And on the morrow he took the four-and-twenty ladies and their horses and raiment and what wealth and jewels had come with them, and he journeyed, and they with him, to Arthur's court. And a welcome had Arthur given him before when he lost him, and a greater welcome now. And of those ladies, she who desired to remain in Arthur's court might have her wish, and she who wished to depart might take her leave.

And Owein remained in Arthur's court from that time forth, as captain of the war-band, and beloved of him, until he went to his own possessions. Those were the Three Hundred Swords of Cenferchyn and the Flight of Ravens. And wherever Owein went, and they with him, he would be victorious.

And this tale is called the Tale of the Lady of the Fountain.

The Dream of Macsen Wledig

Macsen Wledig[1] was Emperor of Rome, and he was the handsomest and wisest of men, and the best fitted to be emperor of all that had gone before him. And one day he held an assembly of kings, and he said to his friends, 'To-morrow,' said he, 'I intend to go a-hunting.' On the morrow early he set out with his retinue and came to the valley of a river which runs down towards Rome. He hunted the valley till it was mid-day. Moreover, there were with him two-and-thirty crowned kings, his vassals at that time. Not for the joy of hunting did the emperor hunt with them so long, but because he had been made a man of such high dignity that he was lord over all those kings.

And the sun was high in heaven above their heads, and the heat great. And sleep came upon him, and his chamberlains set their shields about him on their spear shafts, as a ward against the sun; they set a gold-

[1] Wledig, gwledig: ruler or prince.

chased shield under his head, and in this wise Macsen
slept.

And then he saw a dream. The dream that he saw
was how he was making along the river valley towards
its upper reaches; and he came to the highest mountain
in the world. He thought the mountain was as high as
heaven; and as he came over the mountain he could
see how he was traversing the fairest and most level
regions that mortal had ever seen, on the far side of
the mountain. And he saw great wide rivers making
from the mountain to the sea, and he journeyed
towards the sea-fords on the rivers; however long he
was journeying so, he came to the mouth of a river,
the greatest any one had seen. And he saw a great city
at the mouth of the river, and in the city a great castle,
and he saw many great towers of various colours on
the castle. And he saw a fleet at the mouth of the river,
and that was the biggest fleet that mortal had ever
seen. And amidst the fleet he saw a ship; and bigger
was that by far and fairer than all the others. And
what he might see of the ship above water, one plank
he saw of gold, and the next of silver. He saw a bridge
of walrus-ivory from the ship to the land, and he
thought how he came along the bridge on to the ship.
A sail was hoisted on the ship, and away she went
44 over sea and ocean. He saw how he came to an island,

the fairest in the whole world, and after he had traversed the island from sea to answering sea, even to the uttermost bound of the island, he could see valleys and steeps and towering rocks, and a harsh rugged terrain whose like he had never seen. And from here he saw in the sea, facing that rugged land, an island. And between him and that island he saw a country whose plain was the length of its sea, its mountain the length of its woodland. And from that mountain he saw a river flow through the land, making towards the sea. And at the river mouth he could see a great castle, the fairest that mortal had ever seen, and the gate of the castle he saw open, and he came to the castle. Inside the castle he saw a fair hall. The roof of the hall he thought to be all of gold; the side of the hall he thought to be of glittering stones, each as costly as its neighbour; the hall doors he thought to be all gold. Golden couches he saw in the hall, and tables of silver. And on the couch facing him he could see two auburn-haired youths playing at gwyddbwyll.[2] A silver board

---

[2] Gwyddbwyll: not, as hitherto translated, chess (a battle-game), but a hunt-game, like the Icelandic *hnefatafl*. Like chess, however, it was played with a board and pieces. The king, from the centre of the board, tries to break through to the safety of the outer edge; the hunting party (without a king) endeavours to pen him in and capture him.

he saw for the gwyddbwyll, and golden pieces thereon. The garments of the youths were of pure black brocaded silk, and frontlets of red gold holding their hair in place, and sparkling jewels of great price therein, rubies and gems alternately therein, and imperial stones. Buskins of new cordwain on their feet, and bars of red gold to fasten them.

And at the foot of the hall-pillar he saw a hoary-headed man seated in a chair of ivory, with the images of two eagles in red gold thereon. Armlets of gold were upon his arms, and many gold rings on his hands; and a golden torque about his neck, and a golden frontlet holding his hair in place; and his presence august. A board of gold and gwyddbwyll before him, and in his hand a rod of gold, and hard files. And he was carving men for gwyddbwyll.

And he saw a maiden sitting before him in a chair of red gold. No more than it would be easy to look on the sun when it is brightest, no easier would it be than that to look on her by reason of her excelling beauty. Vests of white silk were upon the maiden, with clasps of red gold at the breast; and a surcoat of gold brocaded silk upon her, and a mantle like to it, and a brooch of red gold holding it about her; and a frontlet of red gold on her head, with rubies and gems on the frontlet, and pearls alternately, and imperial stones;

and a girdle of red gold around her; and the fairest sight to see of mortal kind.

And the maiden arose to meet him from the chair of gold, and he threw his arms around the maiden's neck, and they both sat down in the chair of gold. And the chair was not straiter for them both than for the maiden alone.

And when he had his arms around the maiden's neck, and his cheek against her cheek, what with the dogs straining at their leashes, and the shoulders of the shields coming against each other, and the spear shafts striking together, and the neighing and the stamping of the horses, the emperor awoke. And when he awoke neither life nor existence nor being was left him, for the maiden he had seen in his sleep. Not one bone-joint of his was there, not the middle of a single nail, to say nothing of a part that might be greater than that, but was filled with love of the maiden. And then his retinue said to him, 'Lord,' said they, 'it is past time for thee to take thy meat.' And then the emperor mounted his palfrey, the saddest man that mortal had ever seen, and made his way towards Rome.

And he was thus the whole week. Whenever the retinue went to drink wine and mead out of golden vessels, he went not with any of them. Whenever they went to listen to songs and entertainments, he went not with them; and nothing could be got from him save sleep. As often as he slept he could see in his sleep the woman he loved best; but when he was not sleeping he cared for naught because of her, for he knew not where in the world she was.

And one day a chamberlain spoke to him, and, chamberlain though he was, he was king of the Romani. 'Lord,' said he, 'thy men all speak ill of thee.' 'Why do they speak ill of me?' said the emperor. 'Because they get from thee neither message nor answer, such as men get from their lord. And that is the reason thou art ill-spoken of.' 'Why, man,' said the emperor, 'do thou bring around me the wise men of Rome, and I will tell why I am sad.'

And then the wise men of Rome were brought around the emperor, and he said, 'Wise men of Rome,' said he, 'a dream have I seen. And in the dream I saw a maiden. Neither life nor existence nor being is there in me for that maiden.' 'Lord,' said they, 'since thou hast entrusted us to counsel thee, counsel thee we will. And this is our counsel to thee: to send messengers for three years to the three divisions of the earth, to seek thy dream. And since thou knowest not what day, what night, good tidings may come to thee, that much hope shall sustain thee.'

Then the messengers journeyed till the end of the year, wandering the world, and seeking tidings concerning the dream. When they returned at the end of the year they knew not one word more than on the day they set out. And thereupon the emperor grieved to think that he should never get tidings of the lady he loved best.

And then said the king of the Romani to the emperor, 'Lord,' said he, 'go forth to hunt the way thou sawest thyself go, whether to the east or to the west.' And then the emperor went forth to hunt and came to the bank of the river. 'It was here,' said he, 'that I was when I saw the dream, and towards the river's upper reaches westwards was I journeying.'

And thereupon thirteen men set forth as messengers of the emperor. And before them they saw a huge mountain which they thought touched heaven. Now this was the guise in which the messengers journeyed: one sleeve there was on the cape of each one of them to his front, in token that they were messengers, so that through whatever warring land they might journey, no harm would be done them. And as they crossed that mountain, they could see wide level regions, and great wide rivers flowing through them. 'Lo,' said they, 'the land our lord saw.'

They journeyed towards the sea-fords on the rivers till they came to a great river which they saw making towards the sea, and a great city at the mouth of the river, and in the city a great castle, and great towers of various colours on the castle. They saw the biggest fleet in the world at the mouth of the river, and one ship which was bigger than any of the others. 'Lo, once more,' said they, 'the dream which our lord saw.' And in that big ship they voyaged over the sea and came to the Island of Britain. And they traversed the Island till they came to Eryri. 'Lo, once more,' said they, 'the rugged land which our lord saw.' They pressed forward till they could see Môn facing them, and till they could see Arfon likewise. 'Lo,' said they, 'the land our lord saw in his sleep.' And Aber Seint they saw, and the castle at the mouth of the river. The gate of the castle they saw open. They came into the castle. Inside the castle they saw a hall. 'Lo,' said they, 'the hall our lord saw in his sleep.' They came into the hall. They saw the two youths playing gwyddbwyll on the golden couch, and they saw the hoary-headed man at the foot of the pillar, in the ivory chair, carving the men for the gwyddbwyll. And they saw the maiden sitting in a chair of red gold.

Down on their knees went the messengers. 'Empress of Rome, all hail!' 'Ah, good sirs,' said the maiden, 'I see on you the mark of high-born men, and the badge of messengers. What mockery do you make of me?' 'No mockery, lady, do we make of thee. But the emperor of Rome hath seen thee in his sleep. Neither life nor existence has he because of thee. A choice thou shalt have of us, lady, whether to come with us, to be made empress in Rome, or the emperor to come hither and take thee to wife.' 'Ah, good sirs,' said the maiden, 'I doubt not what you tell me, nor on the other hand do I overmuch believe it. But if 'tis I whom the emperor loves, then let him come hither to fetch me.'

And by day and by night the messengers sped them back, and as their horses failed they left them and purchased others anew. And when they reached Rome they greeted the emperor and asked for their reward, and that they obtained even as they named it. 'We will be thy guide, lord,' said they, 'by sea and land, to the place where that lady is whom thou lovest best. And we know her name, her kindred, and her lineage.'

And straightway the emperor set out with his host, and those men as their guide. Towards the Island of Britain they came, over sea and ocean, and he conquered the Island from Beli son of Manogan and his sons, and drove them into the sea. And he came straight on to Arfon; and the emperor recognized the land the moment he saw it. And the moment he saw the castle of Aber Seint, 'See yonder,' said he, 'the castle wherein I saw the lady I love best.' And he came straight to the castle and into the hall, and there he saw Cynan son of Eudaf and Gadeon son of Eudaf playing at gwyddbwyll. And he saw Eudaf son of Caradawg sitting in a chair of ivory, carving pieces for the gwyddbwyll. The maiden he had seen in his sleep he saw sitting in the chair of red gold. 'Empress of Rome,' said he, 'all hail!' And the emperor threw his arms around her neck. And that night he slept with her.

And on the morrow early the maiden asked for her maiden fee, because she had been found a maid; and he asked her to name her maiden fee. And she named for her father the Island of Britain from the North Sea to the Irish Sea, and the three adjacent islands, to be held under the empress of Rome, and that three chief strongholds be made for her in the three places she might choose in the Island of Britain. And then she chose that the most exalted stronghold should be made for her in Arfon, and soil from Rome was brought there so that it might be healthier for the emperor to sleep and sit and move about. Later the other two strongholds were made for her, none other than Caer Llion and Caer Fyrddin.

And one day the emperor went to Caer Fyrddin to hunt, and he went as far as the top of Y Frenni Fawr, and there the emperor pitched his tent. And that camping-ground is called Cadeir Facsen from that day to this. Caer Fyrddin, on the other hand, was so named because the stronghold was built by a myriad men.[3]

Thereafter Elen thought to make high roads from one stronghold to another across the Island of Britain. And the roads were made. And for that reason they are called the Roads of Elen of the Hosts, because she was sprung from the Island of Britain, and the men of the Island of Britain would not have made those great hostings for any save for her.

Seven years was the emperor in this Island. Now it was the custom of the Romans at that time, that whatever emperor should stay in foreign parts a-conquering seven years, he must remain in that conquered territory, and not be permitted to return to Rome. And then they made them a new emperor. And then that emperor drew up a letter of threat to Macsen. It was moreover no more of a letter than: IF THOU COME, AND IF EVER THOU COME TO ROME. And that

[3] Caer Fyrddin. The name has nothing to do with myrdd, 'myriad'. It is the old Maridunum, the modern Carmarthen.

letter and the tidings came all the way to Caer Llion to Macsen. And thence he in return sent a letter to the man who said he was emperor in Rome. In that letter too there was nothing save: AND IF I GO TO ROME, AND IF I GO.

And then Macsen set out with his host for Rome, and France he conquered, and Burgundy, and all the countries as far as Rome, and he laid siege to the city of Rome.

A year was the emperor before the city; his taking it was no nearer than on the first day. But behind him came brothers of Elen of the Hosts from the Island of Britain, and a small host with them, and better fighters were in that small host than twice their number of the men of Rome. The emperor was told how the host was seen dismounting near his own host and pitching its tents, and never had mortal seen a host handsomer or better furnished or with braver standards for its size than that was. And Elen came to look on the host, and she recognized her brothers' standards. And then came Cynan son of Eudaf and Gadeon son of Eudaf to visit the emperor, and the emperor welcomed them and embraced them.

And then they watched the Romans assault the city. And Cynan said to his brother, 'We shall seek to assault the city more cannily than this.' And then they measured by night the height of the rampart, and they sent their carpenters to the forest, and a ladder was made for every four of their men. And when they had those ready, every day at mid-day the two emperors would take their meat, and on both sides they would cease fighting till all had finished eating. But the men of the Island of Britain took their meat in the morning, and drank till they were inspirited. And while the two emperors were at meat the Britons approached the rampart and planted their ladders against it. And forthwith they went in over the rampart. The new emperor had not time to take up arms before they fell on him and slew him, and many along with him. And three nights and three days were they subduing the men who were in the city and conquering the castle, and another company of them guarding the city lest any of Macsen's host should come inside until they had subdued all to their will.

And then Macsen said to Elen of the Hosts: 'It is a great marvel to me, lady,' said he, 'that it was not for me thy brothers should conquer this city.' 'Lord emperor,' she answered, 'my brothers are the wisest youths in the world. Now go thyself to ask for the city, and if they are masters of it thou shalt have it gladly.' And then the emperor and Elen came to ask for the city. And then they told the emperor that taking the city and bestowing it upon him was the concern of none save the men of the Island of Britain. And then the gates of the city of Rome were opened, and the emperor sat on his throne, and all the Romans did him homage.

And then the emperor said to Cynan and Gadeon, 'Good sirs,' said he, 'I have gained possession of all my empire. And this host I give you to conquer what region of the world you will.' And then they set out and conquered lands and castles and cities, and they slew all their men, but the women they left alive. And in this wise they continued until the youths who had come with them were hoary-headed men with the length of tiume they had been about that conquest. And then Cynan said to Gadeon his brother, 'Which wilt thou,' said he, 'remain in this land or go to the land from whence thou art sprung?' So he determined to go to his own land, and many along with him; but Cynan and another company stayed on to live there. And they determined to cut out the tongues of the women, lest their language be corrupted. And because the women were silenced of their speech, and the men spoke on, the men of Llydaw were called Brytanieid.[4]

[4] The derivation of Llydaw (Brittany) implied in this sentence is from lled, 'half', and taw, 'silent'. An onomastic tale again.

And thence there often came, and still come from the Island of Britain, men of that tongue.

And this tale is called the Dream of Macsen Wledig, emperor of Rome. And here is an end of it.

Phoenix 60p Paperbacks

History/Biograpy/Travel

The Empire of Rome A.D. 98–190 *Edward Gibbon*
The Prince *Machiavelli*
The Alan Clark Diaries: Thatcher's Fall *Alan Clark*
Churchill: Embattled Hero *Andrew Roberts*
The French Revolution *E.J. Hobsbawm*
Voyage Around the Horn *Joshua Slocum*
The Great Fire of London *Samuel Pepys*
Utopia *Thomas More*
The Holocaust *Paul Johnson*
Tolstoy and History *Isaiah Berlin*

Science and Philosophy

A Guide to Happiness *Epicurus*
Natural Selection *Charles Darwin*
Science, Mind & Cosmos *John Brockman, ed.*
Zarathustra *Friedrich Nietzsche*
God's Utility Function *Richard Dawkins*
Human Origins *Richard Leakey*
Sophie's World: The Greek Philosophers *Jostein Gaarder*
The Rights of Woman *Mary Wollstonecraft*
The Communist Manifesto *Karl Marx & Friedrich Engels*
Birds of Heaven *Ben Okri*

Fiction

Riot at Misri Mandi *Vikram Seth*
The Time Machine *H. G. Wells*
Love in the Night *F. Scott Fitzgerald*